JIMMIE JOHNSON

Nicole Pristash

New York

Published in 2009 by The Rosen Publishing Group, Inc.
29 East 21st Street, New York, NY 10010

First Edition

Book Design: Michael J. Flynn
Layout Design: Kate Laczynski
Photo Researcher: Jessica Gerweck

Photo Credits: All images © Getty Images, Inc.

Library of Congress Cataloging-in-Publication Data

Pristash, Nicole.
  Jimmie Johnson / Nicole Pristash. — 1st ed.
      p. cm. — (NASCAR champions)
  Includes index.
  ISBN 978-1-4042-4447-4 (library binding) ISBN 978-1-4042-4543-3 (pbk)
  ISBN 978-1-4042-4561-7 (6-pack)
  1. Johnson, Jimmie, 1975– —Juvenile literature. 2. Stock car drivers—United States—Biography—Juvenile literature. I. Title. II. Series.
  GV1032.J54P75 2009
  796.72092—dc22
  [B]
                                              2007047423

Manufactured in the United States of America

Contents

Jimmie Johnson is a race car driver for NASCAR. Jimmie started racing **motorcycles** when he was four years old.

4

5

Soon, Jimmie began racing trucks in off-road races. Later, he decided to race cars instead.

In 2002, Jimmie started racing in the Winston Cup.

Jimmie won three races his **rookie** year in the Winston Cup Series. He finished fifth in NASCAR's **rankings**.

11

Jimmie Johnson's racing number is 48. Lowe's sponsors his car. This means Lowe's helps pay for the car and keeps it going fast.

13

After Jimmie's rookie year ended, he kept getting better. Jimmie finished in second place in 2003 and 2004.

15

Jimmie's best year was 2006. He won the Daytona 500 and the Nextel Cup **championship** that year!

16

Jimmie often holds **golf tournaments**. They raise money for groups that help build houses for the poor.

18

In 2007, Jimmie won the Nextel Cup championship for the second time. He hopes to stay at the top for years to come.

20

JIMMIE JOHNSON 48

NASCAR NEXTEL CUP SERIES

CHAMPION

21

Glossary

championship (CHAM-pee-un-ship) A race held to decide the best, or the winner.

golf (GOLF) A game in which players use clubs to hit a small white ball into a hole.

motorcycles (MOH-tur-sy-kelz) Two-wheeled machines on which people ride.

rankings (RAN-kingz) Guides to how well a player is doing in a sport.

rookie (RU-kee) A new player or driver.

series (SIR-eez) A group of races.

tournaments (TOR-nuh-ments) Groups of games to decide the best player.

Books and Web Sites

Books

Kelley, K.C. *NASCAR: Daring Drivers*. Pleasantville, NY: Reader's Digest, 2005.

Lovitt, Chip. *NASCAR: First to the Finish*. Pleasantville, NY: Reader's Digest, 2004.

Web Sites

Due to the changing nature of Internet links, the Rosen Publishing Group, Inc., has developed an online list of Web sites related to the subject of this book. This site is updated regularly. Please use this link to access the list: www.powerkidslinks.com/nascar/johnson/

Index